Days

OTHER TITLES IN THE HEBN FRONTLINE SERIES

Upper Level

Cyprian Ekwensi: *For A Roll of Parchment*
Patrick Fagbola: *Kaduna Mafia*
Niyi Osundare: *The Eye of the Earth* (Joint-Winner of the 1986
Commonwealth Poetry Prize)
Rose Njoku: *Withstand the Storm*
Jeremiah Essien: *In the Shadow of Death*
Okinba Launko: *Minted Coins*: (Winner of the Africa Zone of 1988 Dillions Commonwealth Poetry Prize)
Chinua Achebe: *Anthills of the Savannah*
Tess Onwueme: The *Reign of Wazobia and other Plays*
Atabo Oko: *The Secret of the Sheik*
Tess Onwueme: *Legacies* (a play)
Niyi Osundare: *Songs of the Season* (poems)
Niyi Osundare: *Midlife* (poems)
Niyi Osundare: *Horses of Memory* (poems)
Afolabi A Adio-Moses: *Flashes of Ideas and Reflections (poems)*
Tolu Ajayi: *The Ghost of a Millionaire*
Oladele Akadiri: *A Sin in the Convent*
Bridget Nwankwo: *Drums of Destiny*
Iyorwuese H. Hagher: *Mulkin Mata* (a play)
Sola Osofisan: *Darksongs* (Winner, 1990 ANA Poetry Prize)
Sola Osofisan: *The Living and The Dead* (Winner, 1990 ANA Prose Prize)
Femi Osofisan: *Once Upon Four Robbers* (a play)
Femi Osofisan: *Yungba Yungba and the Dance Contest*
Stella Oyedepo: *Beyond the Dark Tunnel* (a play)
Chukwuemeka Ike: *The Search*
Chukwuemeka Ike: *The Naked Gods*
Chukwuemeka Ike: *The Chicken Chasers*
Stella Oyedepo: *The Greatest Gift* (a play)
ANA/British Council: *Five Plays* (Winner, 1989 ANA Drama Prize)

Patrick Idahosa: *Truth and Tragedy*
Chidi Ikonne: *Our Land*
Rasheed Gbadamosi: *Sunset Over Nairobi*
Femi Osofisan: *Aringindin and the Nightwatchmen*
Omowunmi Segun: *The Third Dimple* (Winner, 1991 ANA Prose Prize)
Phanuel Akubueze Egejuru: *The Seed Yams Have Been Eaten*
Ralph Opara: *It Never Happened to Me*
I.N.C. Aniebo: *Rearguard Actions* (Winner, 1998 ANA Prose Prize)
John Munonye: *A Kind of Fool*
Akinwumi Isola: *Madam Tinubu* (play)
Lupenga Mphande: *Crackle at Midnight* (poems)
Tanure Ojaide: *Invoking the Warrior Spirit* (poems)
Charles Bodunde: *Nectar Pots* (poems)
Kunle Ajibade: *Jailed for Life*
Wale Okediran: *Strange Encounters*
Osi Ogbu: *The Moon Also Sets*

Intermediate Level

Chinelo Achebe: *The Last Laugh and Other Stories*
Tess Onwueme: *Ban Empty Barn and Other Plays*
Tess Onwueme: *Mirror for Campus* (a play)
Tess Onwueme: *The Trial of the Beautiful Ones* (a play)
S. Arogbofa: *Agidi Sours* (a play)
S. Arogbofa: *A Celebration of Love*
S. Arogbofa: *A Game of Power*
Ola Rotimi: *A Tragedy of the Ruled* (a play)
F. Aig-Imoukhuede: *Pidgin Stew and Sufferhead* (poems)
Kathleen Egbuna: *That Wartime*
M. J. Akpabio: *A Trip to the Atlantic*
T. M. Aluko: *First Year at State College*
Tony Marinho: *The Epidemic*
Clement Okosun: *A Child with a Child*
Cyprian Ekwensi: *Motherless Baby*
Felicia Onyewadume: *First Term at School*

Felicia Onyewadume: *Echoes of Hard Times and other plays*
Adenike Akinjobi: *Family Secrets (a play)*
Dance of the Maidens

Junior Level

A.O. Oyekanmi: *The Lion and the Hare*
Augustus Adebayo: *Once Upon a Village*
Chinua Achebe: *Chike and the River*
Chinwe M. Agbakoba: *Mma and Nkita*
Chinwe M. Agbakoba: *Ejiofor and His Mother*
Margaret Brook: *The Play for Yejide*
Cyprian Ekwensi: *Gone to Mecca*
Cyprian Ekwensi: *Passport of Mallam Ilia*
Cyprian Ekwensi: *Trouble in Form Six*
Cyprian Ekwensi: *Tortoise and the Brown Monkey*
Olufunmilayo Oyelese: *Where is the Princess?*
Tony Marinho: *Bobo Learns to Fly*
Tony Marinho: *Tell it to Mr. President*
Jasper Onuekwusi: *A Son Among Daughters*
Chio Enwonwu: *Tortoise in Exile*
Chio Enwonwu: *Tortoise Goes to Town*
Chio Enwonwu: *Tortoise Returns to the Woods*
Remi Adedeji: *Stories my Mother told me*
Ernest Emenyonu: *Uzo Remembers His Father*
Olajire Olanlokun: *The Mystery Woman of Aporo*

Beginners' Level

Gabriel Okara: *Little Snake and Little Frog*
Chinua Achebe & John Iroaganachi: *How the Leopard Got its Claws*
Gabriel Okara: *An Adventure to Juju Island*
Mabel Segun: *The Twins and the Tree Spirits*
Olajire Olanlokun: *The Ladder Trap*

Days

Niyi Osundare

HEBN Publishers Plc

HEBN Publishers Plc
Head Office: 1 Ighodaro Road, Jericho, P.M.B. 5205, Ibadan
Phone: (02) 2412268, 2410943, 2411213; *Fax:* (02) 2411089, 2413237
E-mail: info@hebnpublishers.com
hebnpublishers@yahoo.com
Website: http://www.hebnpublishers.com

Area Offices and Branches
Abeokuta . Abuja . Akure . Bauchi . Benin City . Calabar . Enugu
Ibadan . Ikeja . Ilorin . Jos . Kano . Katsina . Maiduguri . Makurdi
Minna . Owerri . Port Harcourt . Sokoto . Uyo . Yola . Zaria

ISBN: 978-9-7808106-72

© Niyi Osundare 2007
First published 2007

All Rights Reserved

No part of this publication may be reproduced, stored in a retrieval system or transmitted in any form or by any means, electronic, mechanical, photocopying, recording, or otherwise, without the prior permission of HEBN Publishers Plc.

This book is sold subject to the condition that it should not by way of trade or otherwise be lent, re-sold, hired out or otherwise circulated without the publisher's prior consent in any form of binding or cover other than that in which it is published and without a similar condition including this condition being imposed on the subsequent purchaser.

Printed by Arin Printers Limited, Ibadan

About the Author

Niyi Osundare Nigerian poet, playwright, essayist, and professor of English; has authored over 15 books of poetry, two books of selected poems, four plays, two books of essays, and numerous scholarly articles and reviews. Among his many prizes are the Association of Nigerian Authors Poetry Prize, the Cadbury/ANA Poetry Prize (which he won on two occasions), the Commonwealth Poetry Prize, the Noma Award **(Africa's most prestigious Book Award)**, and the Fonlon/Nichols Award **for "excellence in literary creativity combined with significant contributions to Human Rights in Africa"**. In 2004, his award-winning book, The Eye of the Earth, was selected as **One of Nigeria's Best 25 Books in the Past 25 Years** by Spectrum Books. He has been recipient of honorary doctorates from l'Universite de Toulouse-Le Mirail in France and Franklin Pierce College, Rindge, USA.

A leading figure in the vanguard for the popularization of written poetry in Nigeria, he maintains a weekly poetry column in Nigeria's Sunday Tribune, and is a frequent contributor to the media on cultural and social matters. He is also a guest columnist for *Newswatch*, a prominent Nigerian news magazine, and an active contributor to public discourse on radio and television. A believer in poetry-as-performance, he has performed his works in many parts of the world, and his poetry has been translated into French, Italian, Slovenian, Czech, Spanish, and Dutch. A fervent campaigner for human rights, social justice, and the environment, he is currently professor of English at the University of New Orleans, USA.

Contents

About the Author viii

Children of the Week

Monday 5
Tuesday 12
Wednesday 16
Thursday 22
Friday 28
Saturday 32
Sunday 39
Epilogue 47
Days Never 48

II
Some Days

Some Days 51

III
Àyájó

Thief of Time 78
Day-do 79
Food Day 80
Between Night and Day 81
Day of the Zebra 82
Odídẹrẹ́ Day 83

Millipede 84
Earthworm 85
Day of the Pigeon 86
Day of the Cat 88
Day of the Baobab 89
Day of the Crossroads 91
Birth Day 93
January 10 95
Aprili 22* 96
April 23, 1564 98
Empire Day 100
Independence Day 102
First Day of Spring 104
Jump Day 105
Day of the Lily 106
Questions 107
Sun on Roof 108
Hunger Days 109
Rich Day, Poor Day 111
I know Days 112
Do Days 113
The Dial 114
Love Day 115
I Envy the Days 116

For Steve Arnold,

Valuable friend

From early days

I

Children of the Week

*(Composed for full orchestration, each day
with a rhythm of its own)*

Monday

You arrived, red-eyed,
Your forehead a wrinkled roster
Of yester-week's unpaid debts
Your feet brown with spent days

Your voice a husky rasp of harvested hours,
On your threshold, visions
Of green dreams and virgin acres
True as the tree which remembers its leaves

True as the cloud which distills its rain
True as the clock ticking in the crossroads
Of tangled moments
True as the winds which unknot their tales

True as the sky's blue laughter
In the journal of a literate noon
Mornings frightened by wild fogs
Noons made bold by a young assertive sun

Oh Monday
January of the working week
Your door is made of featherwood
And stubborn teak

Your fancy frames the winds
Into shadesome spheres;
Jaunty your jamb
Your hinges oiled by the sweat of running days

With Time's trophy held so high
Through the triumphal arch of bended shadows
You carve your keyhole into a periscope
Your window into a vista on sibling days

A tender flame flickers
In the fireplace
Between the silver sky
And a dew-drenched earth

The hearth, damp all these workless hours,
Is aglow with crackling flairs
Ashes stirring
Hearthstones laughing

Sizzle and song
Yawn and yarn
Time for the flame's red rage
In the empire beneath the pot

Time for the lyric's crisp line
In the creased narrative on
The face of a looming week;
For the lilt which comes before the lift

A new day is quivering on its mark
Time for the sun to un-silence its whistle
Behold roads aloud with feet
Costumed corporate clans

Hordes of the Sweat Brigade
Machetes out of their scabbards
Pens out of their pockets
Tongues out of their mouths

Monday masters its shout
And mistresses its shuffle
The house is larger than the street
One corn-grain is a mighty harvest/meal

Monday morning
The week's bell has gone
Birds shake in the trees
Fishes stride across the waters

Lovers hiss at the sun
Beneath their crumpled sheets
Soon the clip clop of donkey hoofs
The yellow blare of crowded buses

Then the whorish bump of chauffeured Benzes. . .
The gateman's hands are a bedlam of keys
Here comes another week,
Ye Labourers of the Land

Hours drag their feet
Like a train of fettered felons

*   *   *

Monday
Spell-bag of myth and mantra:
"No credit to-day", the àkàrà* seller insists,
"Pay up front or leave my buka**";
This is Monday; don't start off my week
With a diary of debts. . .

Alogbo looks out at the street
And beholds a man in rags
He rams shut his window
And dashes for a bowl of water
"I must wash that evil sight from my eyes",

He mutters in prayerful dread;
A mad man is not the best thing
To see on a Monday morning

And Monday takes it all
In its marvelous stride
A flywhisk in its right hand,
In its left a bowl of seedcorns
Its feet sequined in crystal dew
Its head haloed in a hue of pollens

*   *   *

Ajé*** knocks on the door today
Let her enter

Ajé knocks on the door
Embrace him with both hands

Rare guest with selective feet
Cowrie eyes, cheeks of ivory

The one whose whisper is thunder
Whose song is music of shifting tides

Ajé knocks on the door
Let her enter

Blessing here, blight there
Owner of the dappled robe

Vice-royal of vicissitudes
Tossed spin of the crossroads

Ajé knocks on the door
Let him (un)turn the knob

Fat and free in lean seasons
Gorgeous-green in times of drought

Ajé called at dawn today
I heard her voice above the dew

*   *   *

'Where is *Ajé's** house?', the snail asks its shell
'Where does the Wandering One unshoe her feet?

Ajé lives in the thickest forest
She lives on the wildest mountains

He lives in the deepest oceans
She lives in the hardest rocks

He lives in the puking cradle
She lives in the tomb

She lives in between earth and sky
He lives at the crossroads

He lives in the lover's smile
She lives in the bosom of the bride

He lives in the sword's command
She lives in the harmony of the harp

She parades the streets in a hammock of honey
He loiters around the lanes draped in blood

*   *   *

The market lives in Monday's mouth
His jaws are crowded with words and wares
Swelling traffic of feet and haggling voices

Days

Seen, unseen,
The living custom their way with the dead
The living-dead hanging light on the thresh

Hold of eerie barters. Skeletons rump around
In borrowed flesh, the stalls brimming
With walking wares. Golden silences hover

Above the blast of crashing prices.
Staccato rainbow is the song of the marketplace,
The Crossroads Prince supervises the Babel of bargains

Monday's road is long
Its feet come with many toes
Day of the cowrie, day of the coin,

Day of crispy notes quarreling for space
In the pocket of the strong-armed.
Hungry hours haggle over

The price of every second
The week empties the stalls
Of remaindered days.

*   *   *

Yes, Monday is my name
I am the Spirit of Nervous Starts
And Mysty Wanderings
Some call me the early bird of the week

Some say I am the aboriginal error
Of their days of toil
Some call me Sunday's unfinished business
Some say I am the bell-boy with golden chimes

I am the debtor's dread
And the creditor's delight
Punctual as passion,
I bear a long sack of omens and amens

Toes stubbed on my rock
Bleed all week, awaiting the frantic balm
Of a penitent Friday
(Does anyone really say

My laughter imperils the state?)
I am the pull which comes before the push
The luminous shadow in the threshold
Of the migrant moon

Monday me right
Monday me free
I am the vigilant sentry
At the doorway of your week

Come now, Painter of the fluid, ineffable,
Spread me flush on the calendar of your canvas
Daub my winks, lift my veil,
Muse me bright with your rainbow brush

Coming and going, coming and going
Ostrich in my reach, giraffe in my range
I scatter my eggs across the week
No day has sand enough to bury my head

*Fried bean-ball

**An inexpensive eating place

***In Yoruba, Monday is Ojo Ajé: Money Day, Day of Commerce

Tuesday

And in comes Tuesday
With a bevy of bread and butterflies
Brown-humped, white-bellied,

Soft and moist, the loaves, wrapped and ready
For the children of hungry hours.
And the butterflies tumble in

In their robe of feathers
Sky-green, lake-red, mountain-blue;
Some grey like a flock of flitting groans

Some turquoise like the sweaty salt of the ocean
And the feathers, the feathers,
Those rich robes on the loom of the wing

Bashful, brittle, so seasonally eternal
Their motley congregation in the early
Tuesday of merciful rains

Flying mushrooms in the forest of the sky
Mouths perfumed with the pollens
Of rainbow gardens

But Tuesday is less predictable,
Less perishable, than its butterflies
Its pageant less extravagant,

Its bread not so abrasive
Sometimes here with the early rains of the week,
Sometimes tardy with the harmattan's dust

Tuesday, Monday's younger brother,
And also its elder
But not for you its rush and rave

Its red-eyed somnolence
Its forehead pock-marked with crowded rosters
Monday (so precocious) took us to the craggy top

Of a week unfolding
Tuesday lulls us in the downy valley
Where time's foliage is truly green

And the sun ticks and talks
Like the eye of the roving owl;
Its summons is simple

Its empire without command;
The sun never sets
On the patience of its spell

Here, then, your valley of songs
Verdant undergrowths
A pageant of petals

Soft, light wind which rustles
The beard of the trees
Friendly as a whisper

The river runs here, full and free
Talkative like a sage
The guava, the pineapple,

The sinfully seductive pawpaw
Ripe mangoes peeping through
The leaves like dangling moons

Through a convoy of clouds
The clod, the clay
The lyric of the loam

I am king of lower regions,
Tuesday once declared
The mountain's crest may be

Too high for my humble eyes
But I know the tiniest secret
Of its big and boastful toes

My barn is full
My roster has no place for lean hours
The winsomest of wines, the hugest of yams

Ọbọ̀kún*, bọ̀kọ́tọ**, the scattered tribes of the cow
The incomparable sọkoyọ̀kòtọ̀***, leafy allurer,
Who pampers the middling husband into a heaving hulk

Tuesday, Twistday
The week challenges you to its dance of days
Its shoulder-shaking, rump-rippling brawl

The dialogue of its hips
The laughter of its limbs
Those bread and butterflies

Which blossomed so wild in your early rains
Let them dance now
In the generosity of your span

Twist on, oh Tuesday
The week says to you:
    Be my song

*   *   *

Palm fronds in the sky
Palm fronds in the sky
This day is Victory's day+
Palm fronds in the sky

The battle is broken
War drums have ruptured their membrane
Trampled grass, arise
Your bended days are gone

Vanquished foes yield up their swords
Fear's arrow has lost its head
Guarded missiles boomerang; the brewer
Gets one cupful of his own poison

Night no longer holds its terror
The day its dread; the sun's arms
Swing freely by its side,
The moon strides across the sky

Locusts depart
Birds sing on leafing branches
A hand, truly human, arrives,
Holding up a lamp to the mind of night.

---

*Ọ̀bọ̀kún: *Large fish of the catfish variety; much valued for its taste and 'class'*

**Bọ̀kọ́tọ̀: *Cow foot, a delicacy in some parts of Yorubaland*

***Sọkọyọ̀kọ̀tọ̀: *(Literally: make-the-husband-robust); green leafy vegetable believed to be very nourishing.*

+*Tuesday is Yoruba's Ọjọ́ Ìṣẹ́gun: Day of Victory*

Wednesday

Wednesday walked into my song
Wayword like a griot
Lips laden with wit and whistle
Wizened wisecracks and bearded ballads

Loyal like a latch, older than dust
Narrow waist of the week's hourglass
Fluent in sand and sound
Grain after grain after grain,

Pouring your life's content
Into the wide extremity
Of a promiscuous week
Hours howl past

Minutes murmur into moments
While the wink plays second fiddle
In the orchestra of transient eternities
The crickets still cricketing in the fields

The stars still peeping through the dark hole
In the door of the sky
Trembling behind their twinkles
Their rabbit ears flapping

Like satellite masts
Fruits ripen half-way in the trees
Showers hang half-way between earth and sky.
The moon's smile half-way between her lips

The market half-way full, half-way empty,
Matrons the movement of its motley mass.
Streams swell into rivers
Little ponds into seamless lakes

Grain after grain after grain

The hunter's undergarment blooms
Into a robe
Boy-day bodies into man-week
Oh middleman of the seven-bear squad

Mind my left
Mind my right
Hold the vital center of my living days
Let my back know

What my front is doing
Prosper my trade
Unclog my path
Let my wares find a throng of buyers

Grain after grain after grain

You wed many things besides
The heart of days
Your ash cools the hearth
After its baptism of fire

Grey, loosely grey,
Fluent as a flurry of flour
Clamorous echoes of yester-fires
Tinder

Spark
The wood's crackling anthem
Stone red raw
Heart(h)stone red raw

Glowing gallantly
Sizzling coquettishly beneath
The teasing pot
And the flames

Towering above the roof
Telltale hints riding skywards
Riding skywards
This ash day

This Day of Ashes
Grey and grim
The soft, silent song
Which epilogues the drama of the blaze

Grain after grain after grain

Ash Day
Lean heir to Tuesday's rotund indulgence
Grey belch from a hardly remembered feast

Here stand we
Under the penny-tent of sins
So ancient they creak in their joints

Toothless from the jaw-breaking "halleluyah!"
Of gullible tribes
The praying mantis mocks the day

On bended knees
Its hands stretched palm-to-palm
Like those of a pleading monk

The leaves Easter-green, passion-soaked,
Drip purple piety on a crosswood
Unriddled with nails

Grain after grain after grain

Between one day too brief for its span
And another too tall for its tale,
In the ashen silence between the hours,

Wondrous Wednesday, here you are,
The sky beneath your feet
Earth above your head

You walk way out west to reach the east
The week ripening, ripening beyond your reach
You mid-song of its pre-harvest

Median pendulum of its giant clock
The week's laughter hangs between your teeth
Eat it with care

Middle finger of its crowded hand
Grab your share
Of the patrimony of the palm

Grain after grain after grain

*   *   *

You who trample the grass
Who behead the tree;
You who think the ash
Is cemetery of the blaze

Behold a new dew dawning
New rains falling
Treetops aflame with fresh buddings
Floral fiesta, flotilla of fragrances

The day has woken
Night has slept;
From the yeast of years
The spore of brittle moments

A century-old ash
Still simmers in the fireplace
The ash is mother of the blaze
The week is daughter of the day

*   *   *

Ojó rú
Ojó rù*

The day which sprouted
On the twig of the moon
Feeds passing seasons

Seed in the pod
Seed in the pod
Seasoned to a glossy hardness

With an eye which sees beyond the haze
Germ on a journey,
Promise of green things

Laugh in the loft,
Cry in the crypt,
Brown sooth on the wing

Blow in the wind
Blow in the wind
Travel soft spaces

Dare rocky acres
Sing with the stone
Carouse with clay

Winnow the wheat
Unchain the chaff
Wind winnow wind winnow

Window on the wit
Your silence is a song
That echoes across the hills

Memory of the moon
Median wick in the lantern of the week
Burn high and low

Mind your ashen flame
Rise rise now
Proclaim your name.

---

*Yoruba Ojórú is English Wednesday. There is a play on the word 'rú' here to mean 'sprout' or rù 'carry', with the primary connotation of 'eeru, ashes.

Thursday

Thunder-day
Child of roaring skies
Whose tongue rattles the roofs

Unjambs the door
Seizes the season's ear
With the music of its fire

Orógbó* eyes
Cheeks of ripened kola
Porridge of a thousand years

Which still burns the fingers
Indigo is your pride
Indigo the oblong summons of your drum

The shoulder-shaking, rib-rapping
Frenzy of your dance
Nifty athletics of your legs

Which tease the dust
Rake the hours
Blue, deep blue, the summons

Of your drum
Which disturbs the spheres
Eavesdrops on the moon

Embrace the solar laughter
Of lingering moments
Slim as lightning

Slim as the sudden serpent
In the blue grass of the sky
Streak-savvy

Parting the dark lips of playful nights
Raking scattered hours
Teasing the ivory speed

On the nails of fleeing toes.

Thursday
Tall as a tale
Fourth finger of the week's crowded hand

Aluminum knuckles
Flesh of flint
Tall day

Tall spaces
Tall showers
Tall suns

Tall span between
Tender dawn and mellow dusk
So many minute rooms

In the house of the hour
So many seconds in the first wink
Of its ticking eye

From moment to momentum
From one little lyric of a lake
To the running epic of mammoth oceans

The day suckled on dawn's dew
Cracked midday kernels
With the steel molars of an adult sun

Greyed with the after-hours
Died into the night
Then the triumphal resurrection

In another dawn, in another name

Thursday
In the awe-ful silence between the claps
Bolts find their braces

The storm settles to a frown
After lightning's serpentine smile
Silence

An electric peace arrests the streets
A raw awe unhinges the door
To the house of memory

Whoever did'nt hear
The wordless conversation of this silence
Its mute magic

Its syllables of sooth
Dripping with every rain
Every raindrop

Slipping through every gap
Of its thickset teeth
White as fear

Brave as a bone
Thread in the seams of parting garments
This brief cessation of sound, of soundings,

These knowing pulsings of fiery breaths.

Blue, deep blue,
The colour of your flair,
Tall day

Thawsday
Sizzling charm in the chill
Of sunless hours

Fourth stanza of the week's rolling song
Melody so generous, so momentous,
Tremulous on the long strings

Of the hour
Booming, booming
On the metallic lips of the rooster's trumpet

Its fiesta of feathers so
Rainbow in the street,
Its comb so pink with pomp

*   *   *

Ojó bó
Ojó bò**

The day which left
    has returned

The day which soared to the skies
    has dropped to the waiting earth

Migrant pebbles of the road
Lift your eyes

Tender *arúwèlè** of the streamside
Wave your hands

No prince, no pauper
No impish emperor heralded by golden trumpets

This day has walked through the moon
And learnt its way

This day has lived with the sun
And borrowed its fire

This day knows the way of the rain
Which knows the way of the river

Gong chimes on the ascent
Ankle bells un-silence the wind

A chorus of beads *wọkọ́ wọkọ́****
On midday's voluptuous waist

Ọjọ́ bọ́
Ọjọ́ bọ́

The day's egg, has dropped from the sky
Yellow fragments hatch into green hours

The day which left has returned
Its feet powdered by silver dust

*   *   *

Oh Thursday
Unleash my sight/lamp
Let me see with your eyes of light

Let me see
Let me see
I will never beat your drum

In the rain
I will never beat your drum
In the rain

Blue, deep blue,
Is the summons of your drum
The stick is bent but not the sound

Beat beat beat
Beat your drum
Beat, Thunderday, beat your drum

The stick is bent but not the sound
The stick is bent
Like a question mark.

*Orógbó is a white, oval-shaped, and bitter kola; special to Sango, God of Thunder
**Ojó bò (the day has returned), Yoruba's name for Thursday. Play on the word 'bò' which could mean 'return' (bọ) or 'drop' (bó)
*** Onomatopoeia: sound of waist beads when rubbed together.

Friday

Pushing Monday beyond the brink
Sprinting past Tuesday like a whirlwind
Leapfrogging over Wednesday
Flying over Thursday's roof
Like a fleeing rogue/comet,
Friday grabs the week by its tail,
A diary of wild finality
And wistful startings.

And the moon, this day, crescent above the trees,
white eyebrow on the darkened forehead of the sky
pock-marked with the scars of spent moons, some banished,
some buried, some bled into blaze, some withering
by the roadside of the sky, some spread-eagled
at the fireplace of chilly nights
some round like the ripe pumpkins of wasted farms
some lean like string beans with swollen joints

And the moon, crescent above the trees,
tame and tender, prim and poor, possessing no wardrobe
for the nudity of its light, no matchstick
to re-live its blaze, virgin vow, true as the sky,
boasting no domes, parading no lofty arcs
no rainbow mats, no fiery scripts on the open
biceps of its faith, yet cynosure of a billion eyes
factor of holy phases

Ancient yet so modern, young and very old
once gone always coming, brink and beginning
Come-go-go-come like the eyes of the ram

tethered to the divine (un)certainty of this day
its stag-like horns, its wistful shoulders
its giant testicles swinging languidly between its legs
East-eyed welcome at the Feast of Rapid Knives
Fast feast, feast fast, this crossroads of

Cross and Crescent, of rough-hewn wood and
blistered shoulders, the whip's dreadful script/scrawl
on the slate of a naked back, the crown of thorns
crimson rivers from the fountain of the ribs,
jabbing insults the cannibal roar of empire
and the hammer and the nail and the rude interruptions
of innocent flesh and Pilate's ponderous prose
and the crimson poetry of last words

*   *   *

Lifeday deathday two-sided like Pilate's penny,
emphatic terminus of the train of the working week
with its freight of fears gallery of goods its screeching hours
its clanging iron *Faka fiki faka fi* its swaying

music its dancing wheels its route iron-narrow, free and
fettered always there. Long road short way. Up up up, village
of the week, here comes Friday (at last) with its train of
surprises *Fakafikifaka fi*. The week's aging tongue

talks to the wind, the wind talks back. Friday is the
faithful interpreter of silent sounds, of unbeaten drums
of villages of voices seeking territories of tongues
of hums hums and hem hems, the lethal lore of quiet letters

Fryday fry-day, how many headless fishes dance in the dread
ful oil of your evening, the firewood of hours glowing red
and rude beneath your pot? How many bended backs sizzle
black and blighted in the vineyard of your vice? How many

whispers die between the lip and the lyric?
Cool (un)clear evenings, anticipated freedom of the after-
hours the week's worries over rosters re-stored to their
racks, hussles harnessed, words resting easy in the hammock

of the tongue, yawns and yells, the nights neon eyes blinking
blinking like excited glow worms, time's wheels
whirring whirring like the will of a stopping train
Short day long night aching drums bravura of popping

bottles vows whose syntax creaks like ageing joints weak-
ended dreams brief halts in the lunar haste. The hours the
hours see how the hours drink the night before fainting
a sea of sinning angels. Behold this purple sunset, this

weak end to a hardy narrative of done days. Behold this
foregone gallop of the horses of memory. And streets draped
in the gossamer wings of fallen termites. And moth-mobbed
lamp-posts mysty like ill-remembered logs

*   *   *

Ojọ́ tí
Ojọ́ tì
Oni lojọ́ Ẹtì*

No road ever runs without its own snare of bends
what will the camel's back be without its hump?
This day, day of darings, running hurdles of hours
A mighty elephant has fallen across the road
Behold the mid-day sun wrestling with a column of shadows
Furtive rays surprise the gloom at the edge of the sky's
mouth falling and rising the day fore-sees the dusk through
the zig-zag streak of lighning's mirror

No rock of silence so hard that it cannot yield to
the double-headed axe of thunder no roof so solid
that it will not rattle from its storm.
No easy day, this day, no easy day:elephant across the road

Flaresmiths, unleash your knives.

*   *   *

Kaka didi kaka di   (rr mm rr m
Kaka didi kaka di   rr dd rr d)

Dance now, lamps of liberated nights. Dance East dance
West. Dance South dance North. Shine like clever pupils
under the luminous headmastery of the stars. A sprawling
week empties into Friday. A frantic Friday has emptied into

the night. Oh night of little hours, un-turban the bottles,
defrock the banquet. Oh drum of easy hours, take possession.
Gather your Crown of Horns.
Sip this cup before Monday's frenetic advent.

**Friday is Ọjọ́ Ẹtì in Yoruba; there is a pun here on the last
syllable 'ti' which could signify difficulty, durability, etc*

Saturday

Bound day
Free day

The cock crows begrudgingly, its comb
Tremulous and wildly voluptuous
Its feathers a raffia thatch over

The dusty roof of its lowly perch
Audible, strangely, the clock, tolling
Every hour, ticking our mortal fears:

The mightiness of the minute,
The sluggish goosestep of a work-(un)free day
Across the waking expanse of the road, the sky

Mists. Yawns and yearnings
Pent-up twitch in the biceps
Rickshaw rattles in the joints

Mattressed dreams rising, rising
Insisting on a place to stand,
On distances to walk

And says the Wizard of the Wee Hours:
Up up up and go
Up up up and go

Don't just dream the world
On your lying back
Grab its grit with your sweating hand

Children of the Week

The bird of the day is far away
Way up there on the tallest tree
Its perch is sure, its flight is free

Its beak is bronze, its feather is gold
Oh so far from the yearning hold
To catch the bird you must try and try

Jump off your feet and learn to fly
Up up up and go and go
Up up up and go and go

The road lies ahead, dense with dew,
Its countenance severe; its spine unspent
Miles of memory, sweeps of insight,

Waiting, waiting for the music of the march...

Between the sleepy hesitation
Of the bed-bound will
And the migrant haste of wayward cravings

The day, dawning, lies,
Riddled with grime and grit.
Muses the Wizard of the Wee Hours again:

"Daring new dawns is no act
For the straw-footed; it is Courage
That rules the territory between

The sleeping chamber and the striving street;
The rarest diamonds live in the dirtiest dust".
Up up up and go and go

    Up up up and go and go. . .

And the amber rays of a mellow morning
Adult into the silver strokes
Of an overarching sun

A noonsome glare unmasks the eyes
Seen and heard the wild tom toms
Of a tropical sky

*   *   *

Sa sa sa ti de*

Run-away day
Day wise with words
Wild with drums

Wild with round-rumped revelers
And their mobile/itinerant mountains
Wild with old songs echoing new

In the streets
Sa sa sa sa ti de
Day which has ample room

For our rituals of excess
Wedding bells coiling into funeral tolls
Diverse ceremonies up with painted faces

Today's right foot is heavy with haze/sin
Its left perfumed by puffs of the powder
Of paradise

Dancing day
Summit of songs
Roofs rock

Treetops sway like masquerades
In a state of trance
Laughters soar in the high heavens

Rainbow wardrobes usurp the streets
Flighty trends drape wild dissipations
In frantic fabrics

Sa ti de
Famished expectations argue
With exuberant hopes

The horse which gallops
On the moon's long road
Looks back at its wondering tail

Then commands: "never say nay!"
Moondrops cure the blisters of the road
Moondrops cure the corn on its smallest toe

The road, this crowded day, has learnt
To walk without stumbling
Heels learn their faces in the mirror

Of polished pebbles
The sole strides through a jungle of tar
Moondrops clip the nail of erring toes

And the hours amble along
Their garments grey with spent moments
Shadows linger

Then climb, up the sky of a vanishing twilight
Homing egrets, echeloned in chalky spaces,
Glide through the hospitality of gracious heights

Hungry smokes rise above the roofs
Political tabernacles gnash their teeth
There is wind in the stomach of their word

*   *   *

Ọjọ́ Àbámẹ́ta**

Today is a crossroads of motions/overtures
Today is a crossroads of motions
Hours hurl in their baggage of wishes

One motion binds Life to the thumb of the sky
One winds Death round the big toe of the sea
Countless others behold Death in the uneven rib

Of Life. Èṣìdálẹ̀ stands on the precipice,
Of mortal options, wondering which path
To plant his foot. Close and very far

Seen and unseen
Short and very tall
Black and egret-white

The Prince of the Crossroads holds court
By the roadside, under the mighty àràbà tree
Draped in silk and flying seeds

The kernel of choice secure
In the labyrinth of his palm.
The sun drinks the rain from the goblet

Of the gods. A rainbow heaves
In the belly of the mid-day sky
The kernel splits; a crimson code is born

This short day is very long
Life's journey winds round its
Branches like a giant cobra.

Right foot first (the left is equally propitious)
A trinity of propositions complicates
The narrative of a crowded day

Saturday may still change its mind
About its place in the divinity of the week

* * *

It being Saturday,
Government is on leave

Justice jostles for space in alleys
And little streets

It being Saturday,
The day evenings into a slow dusk

The night never sleeps
Silence knows what not to do

With its horns of windy absence
Tipsy fingers strum the ribs of the streets

Lamp-posts sway in the dark stupor
Of NEPA*** nescience

It being Saturday,
Nights cough without sneezing

Drink without pissing
Regale lengthy hours with the harmonica

From their wardrobe of winds
The night never sleeps

Sa ti de
An ageing week meanders

Into Sunday's sea
A tableau of tides lays down its tribute

Before a delta of dreams
The day which taught the hours

To cry
Also has a school of laughter

Ah, Sa ti de!

---

*Yoruba pronunciation of 'Saturday', here signifying the idea of running and arriving

** Literally, Day of Three Propositions: Yoruba name for Saturday

*** NEPA: National Electricity Power Authority - notorious for its grossly inefficient service

Sunday

Sunday sits supreme
At the bottom of the diurnal ladder
Young from its midnight coming

Its murmur green as an orchard
Its navel raw from fresh plucking
In its mouth a lode of budding songs

Week dawning
Darkness thawing
Dew crystal crown on the head

Of reluctant grass
Earthworms' charted crossings
In the wilderness of yawning roads

    Breezes crisp like fresh-picked petals

Dawning done
Mist rising rising rising
Like the robes of a wealthy merchant

Glow worms fledge into glow suns
The hearth's tepid flicker
Into the bonfire in the sky

Mist rising rising rising
Sun day
Day of the Sun

Sunday Sun day
What side of your bed saw your rise,
Oh curious day:

Is it Saturday's side
With its empty bottles and staggering gaits?
Is it Monday's

  With its crowded rosters and lingering aches?

Dawning done
Then a banquet of bells
High up in the tower

Or clamorous between the clergy's lips
Leaden vibes in the air in the air
Trembling ears, shuddering bellies

Bellbeat heartbeat bellbeat heartbeat
Sinful angels and holy Satans
Bell ring bell ringing

Faith flowers flourishing in the potted pits
Of sacred eyes
Leaden music of the spheres

Panting planets
Clouds in congress
Restless orbit

Of the eyes of the owl
A whirlwind of wisdom
The dust in ascent

In ascent
   In ascent
      In ascent

The dust in ascent
The wind leaps and lisps
In accents beyond the ear

   The muse
      The muse
         The Music of the Sphere

Angels sing and sway in their chariot of lyre
Above the monks and their sober habits
The dust of silence on the heels of the song

Dawning done
The day is born
Hello Sun

Hail your shine
Your round-faced smile
Your fire-fingered touch

Your glorious glow on mango leaves
The dappled canvass of the forest floor
The hidden fire in the tiger's paws

Mo r'Oṣùmàrè lokè o   (I see the rainbow in the sky
Mo r'Oṣùmàrè lokè   I see the rainbow up high
Òní d dára   Today holds a package of prospects
Oní d dára o   Today holds a package of prospects
Mo r'Oṣùmàrè lokè. .   .I see the rainbow in the sky)

Rain, Sun mating
In a bed beyond the clouds
Rain, Sun mating

The magic and the moan
The shuddering of the heights
A splash of water

A phalanx of light
A wondrous brow on the forehead
Of the sky

The rain and its bow
The rain and its bow
Quivering with de-light

   Quivering
   Quivering
   Quivering with de-light

   Rainbow Rainbow bright and bold
   Where do you keep your pot of gold
   Where where where where
   Where do you keep your pot of gold?

The day walks the streets,
Its feet sequined in minutes and moments
Its head halo-ed in the haze of hours

From stone-cast vaults
A quarry of hymns
And the sins which spy the streets

Behind the stained glass window
Of pastoral seasons
Beneath the wing of captivating angels

Sunday
Sun day
Baobab beams from savannah roofs

And grass slithering through the noon
Like snakes through a forest of ferns
Baobab beams

Prop-rooted girths and giant pods
Thick salutations of sappy seasons
Elephant rumps and rumbling spaces

(No subject for mean encirclements)
Beyond the petty prison of hours
The day stretches its limbs

Walks the streets
Counting every wink in the eye
Of leering houses

(The day bites its nail,
Wondering how to melt into a week
Still in its active infancy)

Sunday
Sun day
Season of the sun

With its yellow roster
Yellow mementoes
Cycles with imperfect O's

Memory drums, faces round like the moon
Which bleeds the sky
Mothering the crowded brood of working days

Oh the orgasmic hip hop of Sunday jumps
Of supple cleavages and bouncing bums
The shrieking arabesque of limbs

    And wrestlers on the grass
    And wrestlers on the grass
    Supine melody of the moan
    Epic poetry of the groan. . .

Flesh flair,
Lair of the lip
Sweat as honey

Tang on the tongue
Oh holy day and its sin-phony of sighs
Angels soaring skywards, their wings

Spotted with sticky tales
Sacred peccadilloes, pagan prophets
And their diocese of I-dols

A fowl-mouthed day unfurls its feathers,
Its clucking so disarming
Its rump a seen thing for playful eyes

Sunday
Sun day
Plumes of prayers fluttering in the wind

Many-hued, bold-toned like
The Rainbow and its Quarry of Gold
Aglow with the week's looming debt

Grim like its grotto of doubt
Welcome, day of light and plume
Sail the week in your flotilla of feathers.

*   *   *

Sunday is cognomen from the sky
Aiku is the name that grew
Like seedcorn from the earth

Green, then brown, with the moons
Plucked off the lips of the wind
Coming and going in deathless motions

Death died on this day
Between Dawn's shy intimations
And the dusken whisper of an expiring sky

Death died on this day
Ashes marched, the dust rose
Rivers leapt skywards in chariots of water

One moon departs
Another moon arrives
The full-throated cock hides

In the yellow peril of the yolk
A musty old rag begets a bale of billowing brocade
Whatever went away is back again

*Aìku l'ojo oni
Kii s'aiku**

Death died today
Ash-coloured claws, relent your grip

Death died today
Wilted leaves, let go of the branch

Death died today
Lurking ailments, depart the shadows

Death died today
Heads, stand tall on your shoulders

Death died today
Oh sun, reclaim the patrimony of the sky

*Today is the day of immortality
Not one that goes without leaving something behind
Aiku is Sunday in Yoruba. The tonal pun here is on 'ku'
which could mean 'die' or 'remain'.

Epilogue

A caravan of days pursues their hours
Their feet so sure

In the sands of hungry shores
Calm as camels

Undulating timewards
Their humps throbbing with memories

The moon-faced clock
Laughs at the sun

Wringing its diamond-tipped hands
In the acre of worsted days

No tears over harried hours
And murdered minutes

The castle of days stands
On the graveyard of moribund moments

How neat the days
In their sequenced silence

How predictable the dynasty of their deeds:
A house dutifully founded by Sunday

    Is roofed by Saturday's assiduous hands

*   *   *

Days Never

Days never lie
Days never cheat
Days never chain the world with iron laws

Days never wear their clothes the wrong way
Never spill sewage words
In the streets of innocent ears

Days never cough
Days never drown a fever
In an ocean of pills

Days never lose their shadows
Days never pay mind-fixers a fortune
To restore their missing chests

Days never ditch you
Because you are different
Days never crush you with a code of colours

Days never curse
Days never cavil
Days never crawl at the feet of power

Days never quarrel with the night
Days never set the sun
In conflict with the moon

II

Some Days

*(To be performed in concatenated flow/rhythm,
like seeds in the pod of the string bean)*

Some Days

i

Some days turn the other cheek
Helplessly mild, for ever meek

Their faces, pock-marked with slaps
They squander the hours under divine wraps

Painstaking, they take all the pain
On their long brows a stubborn strain

Hours scurry under the arc of the whip
A look into their soul is a sobering trip

Minutes mumble in suppressed murmur
As if a scream would provoke a tremour

Seconds slink in rattling rows
In a nervous round of to's and fro's

The rosy cheek with an Eden of dimples
Has become a swathe of sour pimples

ii

some days

like to smile
but have no teeth

some like to dance
but are desperate for legs

some crave the rainbow
but reap the rain

some dwell the desert
and dream the sea

some have a multitude of means
in search of a warrant of ways

some have a sun
in need of a sky

some are so bored by the light
they crave the company of the night

Children of the Week   53

iii

Days of fire
days of fright

atomic seconds
bloom into hydrogen hours

nuclear nannies
embrace their mushroom babies

*(They kill
Therefore, they are)*

First, sack the city
invent reasons later

to justify your act;
if none pops up itself

seek WMD's*
in the skulls of wailing infants

Might is right
Fright is spright

in this Brave New Age
of the Lone Ranger

the end seeks every way
to justify the mean-ness

*Weapon of Mass Destruction

iv

Some days sing your praise
when your sun is high in their sky

they bow to the ground
roll in the dust

worm their way into your
purse en route your heart

share your roof
invade your barn

But when your sun slips
(though temporarily)

behind the clouds
they fold up their mats

change their song
forget your face

Some days are
like the lower jaw

which gobbles up all the delicacies
when you are up and going

and drops fast and fickle
the very moment you breathe your last

Some days
are fair-weather friends

They rob the clouds
to pay the sun

v

Some days unravel the night,
its dreary mask/shrouds bared
to the glaring stars

some arrive
punctual like morning guests
fragments of supple shadows

around their feet
their footsounds loud
their lineaments correct

Sure about their Name
they forage no dusty registers
for cognomens of alien gods

Unwavering about their Song
they pillage no pale temples
for the true latitude of their lyrics

Their tongues no longer
quarrel with their mouths

Their masks have a meaning
beyond the facile phase

vi

Some days drag their feet
across dawn's threshold
hesitant like unwilling brides

their shadows fall behind,
voluminous shawls from
the loom of the moon

Darkness's labour done,
the cradle of light not yet sure
of the heaviness of the breaking day

Some days munch the minutes
so slowly they never make it
through the feast of hours

Every moment arrives
with a mountain yoked to its feet,
every wink with a swathe of worries

Some days slither out of the shell
of dawn, yearning loudly
for the womb of night

Some days are
simply
scared of the nemesis of noon

vii

Some days know what it means

To have
And not to hold

To live life as if on loan
To spy the sky's face

Through the holes
In the roof

To sire a village
And walk the lonely path

To shout
And not be heard

To sow
And not to reap

To love
And not be loved

To seek
And not to find

To perish in wars
Provoked by others

To live beside the river
And die of thirst

To live at noon
Without a shadow

To be
And not to be

viii

Some days face the week
with a forest of frowns

Smiles stumble
on their lips

A clutter of clouds
plays around their brows

Their cheeks swell
like angry boils

Their eyes narrow
like a prowling tiger's

Their bellies are active volcanoes
with a cortege of smokes

On their left
carcasses of murdered mirth

On their right
skulls of yester-joys

Low as serpents
they crawl in their sorrow lanes

Slink from the sight
of the zestful sun

Drip every hour
like mournful sores

Some days know not
the magic power of laughter

ix

Some days
Break rocks with bare hands

Haul oceans of sand
Up impossible mountains

Walk pebbled pathways
Till they bleed in the sole

Trudge through the rain
Burn with the mid-day sun

Ply life's commerce
At a terrific loss

Some days
Return home

Trounced by thunder
Wounded by the wind

Pulled in different quarters
Like carcasses in a jungle of jackals

Skinned at noon
To make drums for Twilight's beloved sun

Some days swim into the night
In the sea of their own sweat

x

Some days
Get the rain

And insist
On the rainbow

Meet the night
And demand the stars

Thresh hunger's hold
For grains of waiting feasts

Rattle History's drum
For hints of hidden echoes

Relieve the scorpion
Of the fire in its tail

Clothe Solitude's bosom
With a strip from Silence's loom

Rock Patience's boat
With one haste and seven angers

Laugh at the storm
With the lyric of the lull

xi

Some days
Are lusty like the lyre

Happy when strummed
With the night's index finger

Sad at the dancers'
Wild, unshod leapings

Melody murmurs
In the corridors of their hearts

Prophecies hurry through
The veins of listening hours

Here now, the vices
Of sceneful gods:

Leering beards
Mustachios wet with fine flaws

Hail the tall wisdom
Of the raffia wine

The sappy fronds which sip
The sun's sinews to the last,

Unholy drop. Avert your gaze,
You, loose, untutored eyes;

Those who have ears,
Let them see

As masked Days
Sip the juice of passing moments!

Bless the sin in every sing
The fame in all blasphemy

xii

Some days
Insist on travelling light

They own no banks
Amass no cars

Gather no wardrobes
Lay no claim to a fleet of houses

Possessions end up
Possessing you, they say

Property weigh you down
Liquidate your equilibrium

xiii

Some days
walk straight

  on their legs
chest out

chin up

lips stiff
    like sentries

feet shod in steel
    eyes made of marble

in the left side
    of their chests

lives an
    absent heart

xiv

Some days
are paved with thorns

minutes murmur
hours limp along

dawns are green
with nettles

noons spiked
with doubts

barbed barricades
unnerve the streets

twlights shop the clouds
for boots of iron

XV

Some days
probe the moon
for secrets of the night

Walk open streets
their strides unsullied
by mean shadows

Encounter History
in a narrow alley
without blinking an eye

Breakfast with fear
dine with doubt
endure unjust desserts

Some days
look into the mirror
and like what they see

xvi

Some days

Are nursed on nostrums
Weaned on the well-worn word
Ready-made like a fast-food fare
Rubbed clean of their sinewy edge

Haughty shibboleths
At the gate of a wary week
They crash through the borders
In fragments and shimmering chips

Strident when silence is gold
Their sillyables dissolve the sun
Plant ticking bombs in the highway
Between the mouth and the ear

Some days
Prattle like packaged proverbs
Flatten rugged wisdom into graded maxims
Predictable like a fool's joke

The demagogue's handy grenade
The politician's promiscuous prop
The hypnotist's incantation
Which puts the sun to bed at noon

Some days
Puke like pocks
Thresh every idiom
For the idiocy of its lineage/pedigree

xvii

Some days
Block their noses
Against the choking stench
Of the ruling wind

    They see no evil
    Hear no evil
    Taste no evil
    Touch no evil

Though every hour
They pick their way
To twilight's temple
Through a Golgotha of groans

Pliable as elephant
Grass in the wind
Pretentious like a mask
Straight out of the devil's wardrobe

They barter conscience
For a piece of compromise
Scourge innocent backs
With blind whips

    Wash their hands
    In a sea of dubious water
    Then wipe their guilt
    On the napkin of the night.

xviii

Some days
lock you up

in the prison
of your skin

lynch you
for your looks

stab your voice
for its strange accent

dim-sighted
they cannot see

beyond the surface
mud-eared

they are for ever deaf to
the summons of the deep

Some days live for ever
In the carapace of colour

xix

Some days see the past
As one dark pit of pain
The future as a bird without a wing

Eyes washed in a sea of clouds
They grope through History's alley
Their soles on thorns

And broken shadows
The sky a shredded shroud
Above their heads

The earth
One mound of messy mush.
Laughter has no room in their house

A cemetery lives in the back-
Yard of their dreams. Their noses
Perch perplexed behind their heads...

Other days see
Through the fog
Beyond the filth

Tough like ancient tales
Their narrative is nous
Their syntax a string of limpid letters

When they see
A tadpole
They dream a frog.

xx

Some days fix their gaze
On the hardly seen:

    the particles of power
    in a sliver of sunlight

    the speck in a spark
    glimpsed at twilight's gorge

    freckles on the face of a termite
    roving eye of the moth

    the cynic's smile
    laughter of the lynx

    ivory spots on the toe-
    nail of a cockroach

    a tiny gesture
    a nifty nod

    a pencil of light
    in the library of night

    a shy hint
    in the hyperbole of the storm

xxi

Some days know
What it means

   to be
   and not to be

   to have a mouth
   but not a tongue

   to own a body
   but not a chest

   to keep on sowing
   and never to reap

   to read your history
   in the conqueror's account

   to fight for every inch
   of the spot beneath your feet

   to be pinned to a corner
   in the castle of your skin

   to knock and knock
   on a deafening door

   to be bitten and bitten
   and asked to be *"never bitter"*

   to cook all the meals
   and choke on crumbs

to live on faith
in a world ruled by force

to shout and not be heard
to be heard and forever ignored

to live without a Name
and a Song to call your own

xxii

Some days feast
So that the world may starve

They lap up the dew
They lick the lakes

They trap the clouds
And rout the rains

They rip the cob
From the loins of the stalk

Whatever lies beneath the sea
Whatever flies above the hills

Whatever rises with the sun
And goes to bed with the moon

Is within their boundless claim
Under their ferocious hammer

They rob the bird of its feather
Debowel the earth for her treasures

Their eyes are big
Their fingers extremely clever

They possess and possess and possess
Till they become the ones possessed

xxiii

(to Akawu)

Some days know
the secret leaning of the heart

their auricles are acres of clay
watered by the kindest dew

their music the beat of every pulse
smiles grow in the garden of their lips

there is grace in their greeting
bliss in their blessing

a merciful moon sits
in the center of their night

their hours ripen
in the shadows of a generous sun

when they pass
houses throw open their doors

flowers drape them
in their rarest fragrance

for them tenderness is no treason
compassion is no constraint

some days
are not allergic to softness

some days
are not afraid of being human

Àyájọ́

To each poem its own rhythm; to all, a harmony

*Special day

Thief of Time

Procrastination steals the day
Dragging its feet like a sleepy schoolboy
Unable to put the morning mist away
In a little corner, like a lingering toy

Tardy and tired, not sure of itself
The day lays by, unknowing where to go
A long, unread book on the week's tall shelf
Draped in dust from head to toe

Time melts away, hour after hour
The sun in the sky will never wait
It plucks the day like a flimsy flower
And drops the year a leaden weight

The thief of time is always on the prowl
It swallows the minutes without a scowl

Day-do

Monday sings a busy song
Crowded with doings and sundry cares
Tuesday's tune is bold and strong
Thursday's thunder is a flurry of flares

Behold Wednesday with its urn of ashes
Its mortal dust, its swathe of grey
In the valley of shadows and summit of flashes
The day weaves fabrics that never fray

Enter Saturday and its chain of chores
A node of means in need of ends
Concourse of plans in tens and scores
All the days are its nervous friends

Famous Friday puts the week to rest
And Easy Sunday is a fleeting guest

Food Day

I'll season the day with a spoon of spice
From backyard gardens and distant seas
My eager tongue knows the dialect of rice
And the frolic of fruits on laden trees

Break of day and I break my bread
Its moist, mellow magic my special treat
Holding life together by delicious thread
With its brown delight, its wisdom and wheat

At noon I call on a pretty yam
Big and crisp and supremely smooth
With dainty stew and leg of lamb
That restore my heart to eternal youth

The busiest room in the house of day
Is surely the kitchen where the treasures lay

Between Night and Day

Between night and day a teasing mystery
Of sunny acres and somber shades
Countless atoms and their chemistry
Of luminous lyrics and their dark parades

Prompt alternations, the settled groove
Dusk dies into night, dawn draws light
The hours clasp their hands with nothing to prove
Their ticking eyes put the day in fright

Wick wack wick wack the hours burn away
Like slick, tall candles ignited by the sun
The shadow's game with the waning day
The millipede seconds for ever on the run

See-saw swings a wondrous pass
Night and day are wrestling in the grass

Day of the Zebra

This is the day of the zebra
running stripes in primal colours
delicate calculations in the algebra
of parallel humours

This is the day of unsullied beauty
of hours roaming wide in the wild
of the sun so mindful of its duty
and ways many and gallantly tried

Liquid symmetry, supreme formation
parallel strokes so close and so apart
a balance of notes in running celebration
the day opens its mind and heart

Like a book in black and white
for dawn to read and write

Odídẹrẹ́ Day

(Flute & shekere)

Roll up your mat, sleepy day
Unfurl your limbs
Odídẹrẹ́ has hit the apron of the moon
Forest leaves, unlatch your larynx
The streamside is a market-
Place of swaying songs

Bird of the Bard
Lend me a touch of your princely pomp
Today is the day of fluff and flair
Land me soft on the wagon of your wing

Clamorous is the eloquence of the hour
Wild, unquenchable is the fire
In the tail of the minute

Polyglot pilgrim
Tease my tongue into feathery tales
Hear-say day, uncurl the question
Mark of your beak
Ayékòótó*, Bird of the Bard,
Tell me clear, tell me quick:
Is the hour scared of the truth
Of the minutes?
Does the forest grudge the trees
For the luster of their leaves?

The world is averse to truth

Millipede

This day belongs to the millipede

Silent locomotive
On the forest track
Brown cylindrical body
Folding up at the slightest touch
Bride so shy
It never looks the groom in the eye
The rain falls
For the comfort of its skin
Streamsides are favourite roosts
In the season of meager drops
Though armed with a million legs
It never tramples its way around
Children hold it in their naked hands
The farmer carries it home
In his inner pocket
Up the tree, down the palm
Across the well-worn path
To the village farm
It wiggles its way without a worry
Slow and steady in its segmented motion
It reaches its goal all the same

Earthworm

(With a solemn Ekòló song)

The day never dawns without its bell
Wriggling string, rosary on the rise
Its song is slime, its veins are
Loud in its transparent skin
Its voice vulnerable, its frame
Fragile as fate
Earth's hardest spot yields
To its 'open' command
It wets the pavement's lips at dawn
But alas, the sun is its mortal foe:
The lukewarm embrace of the morning glow
The merciless grill of the noonday fire
Rootsman,
Farmer's friend
Its covenant with earth is long and deep
It softens the soil for coming harvests.

Day of the Pigeon

(Gong & drums; songs)

Wandering day
Wandering day
Ọsun traverses yawning plains on hidden legs
Minding every patch on the path of hurrying days
Her life flows with gathering hours
Her stomach billows with wind and muddy mists

Behold the sparkling laughter
Of her droplets at noon
When the sun, famished workman,
Lays siege at the water's edge
Its throat hoarse like a husk

Èyékàírè* douses the sun's drought
With a sigh of showers, whispers a few wet winds
In the ears of the blaze and the world regains
The peace of the dew at dawn

Rounded pebbles her waistbeads
Her eyelashes a sorority of *arúwèlè***,
Grinning coquettishly in the early rains
The rhyme and reason of her ribs
Rippling bankwards with a cache of golden sands

Farmer's friend, the hunter's consort
Eternal confidant of the Deity of Chalk and Clay
Mender of lost cracks. Sango+ may set its sky ablaze
And his Lightning flash its torch
Of silver serpents, but who does not know
That water has a cure for the flaming bolt?

Parrot-feather hair, eyes like ripened kola
No baptistery goes beyond her font
The alien zealot who calls her by a vulgar name
Will wash his beads in a bowl of dust
The watercress rides the crest of the tide
Its liquid limbs a delicacy in the midday kitchen
Her herbal pot simmers on the cooling hearth
She who medicines the malady of febrile seasons

Feathery heights, cooing capers
Pigeons in the evening wind
Sacred servants of the Merciful One
Eternal couriers of peaceful tidings
The water meets the wind on her wings
Ọsun fashions little nests from the debris
Of expiring moons

Day mounts day, season speeds past season
She billows on in her soothing majesty,
Seeding clouds, doctoring droughts.

---

*Literally, The-Mother-We-Pet; Ìkẹ́rẹ́ - name for the Goddess of Osun River.
**Fresh, green grass, the type that comes with the rains or is found by the streamside
+Yoruba God of Thunder and Lightning

Day of the Cat

Today jumped down
from the rafter of the sky
a cat, diamond-eyed,

unafraid of the night
paw powdered by the clouds
mane soft like cotton wool

mattressed by the minutes
threshing whatever seeds are left
in the husk of the hour

Feline flowers in memory's garden
a fraternity of fragrances
navigates the estuary of the nose

(I smell, therefore, I know)

Agile day
hungry as an angry claw
the minutes roam the streets

like careless mice
oh cat day,
spare their ribs.

Day of the Baobab

(for Sonja, who sent a postcard)

(Kora, goje, drums)

She knows where the winds achieved their wings
For her house dwells the lip of the desert
Where the Sahel whispers sandy songs

Into the ears of the savannah grass
The rains, when they come, are fragile
Like ethereal droplets, their lineaments

Brown, then grey, before their rapid journey
Into the throat of the waiting dust
Born in the season of meager moons,

Her children have learnt to mould
Blue lakes from the sweat of the sky
And wash their faces with the dew of little stars

Behold her round raptures, her bulbous blessings
Brown with the sun
Grey with eloquent stories of wordless griots

Bamboo clumps fan her face
Cassava roots unshoe her feet
When she sways in the evening air

A masquerade looms in the lengthening shadows
Even as punctual flowers perfume her breath
Her foliage waves its brittle hands

To the homing sun. Elephant legs rooted
Against the tyranny of storms,
She swings through the fog of the hour

To the blue tonality of deathless skies
Still wondering which is older:
   The truth of her beauty

        or

The beauty of that truth
She towers above the mortal fragility
Of the sands, her gaze long, her faith unfazed

Day of the Crossroads

(*Gong, bell, drums; songs*)

What time of day it is
We do not know:

It has the misty intimations of dawn
Though it is already past the twilight zone

Its rainbow is one long quarrel
Between the sun and the lingering rain

At times when you behold its sun
You think it is the moon eating its dinner

The minutes are longer
Than the hours

Shadows lead
Their owners follow

Going West, facing East
This day hits the market in shifting colours

The compass's clever fingers
Betray a riot of routes

Pǫnmbété ponmbété pǫnmbété pǫn
Oríta bítí oríta bàtá
Pǫnmbété ponmbété pǫnmbété pǫn

North rides South
West wrestles East

The wanderer faces the puzzle
Wondering where to go

The hours halt at the crossroads of the sun
A tricky twist to the tale of prancing shadows

Day-farers, mind your toes
There are hidden outcrops on the road

To the house
Of the Prince of Pranks**

* No real semantic 'meaning' used here for its tonal, musical function.

**Oblique reference to Èṣù, the Yoruba god of fate and happenstance

Birth   Day

Crimson moments
Crimson moments*

Bring the bowl
And the camwood cream

Parrot feathers
And the woodpecker's beak

Borrow a quill
From the peacock's plume

Inscribe this day
In ink of gold

Today's sun rose
In a different sky

Murmuring with mountains
Rustling with leaves

Indigo's deep song
In the pot of the sea

The laughter of the lily
In the garden of the sun

Crimson moments
Crimson moments

Mother's fearful joy
Father's mortal pride

Marching moons
And talking clocks

Fleeting shadows
And the steady sky

Restless wheels
Of the rolling year

*Title of Chuks Ihekaibeya's poem: March 12, 1974; Leeds, UK.

January 10

(for the Poetry Club, University of Ibadan)

(With the song:
A ti l'ékú w'ọdò (We have driven Death into the ditch
A ti l'ékú lo   (We have driven Death away)

A rude axe erupted
from night's hidden hand
amid the rustle
of harmattan leaves

And rumble of elephant grass.
A heavy thud
a broken skull
a font of gurgling blood

Death came calling
without a mask
on a small dirt road
with a sandy song

The moon saw it all
behind the clouds
so cruelly shaken
she spilled her milk

Many suns later
before an acre of scars
the bards penned paeans for
"The Poet Who Refused to Die"

Aprili 22*

(To be accompanied with Music of the Earth - in any language)

Everyday is Earth's
Earth is everyday's

But this day is the day
Of the bell and the gong
Of solemn awakenings
And the hurt which comes before the herb

Wounded trees bleed in the forest
Lynched lakes congeal like rancid potions
A poisoned sea foams
At the edge of a million mouths

Who dare forget
The day the River caught fire
And the Mountain lay crushed
Like a mound of hapless cake

Yellow rains, crimson dew,
Broiling winters, freezing summers
A perforated sky leaks red tears
Into the basin of thinning rivers

A tropical madness unclothes the streets
New-born babies surprise the cradle
With double heads. A heartless Science
Has sowed the wind; see how we reap the storm

Where are the silk-petalled flowers
Birds with feathers of paradise
Air clean like the breath of a mountain spring
Dust which speaks the language of the human skin?

This day insists that we

Restore the frog to its pond
The dew to its grass
Man to his mind
Earth to its future

April 23, 1564*

Rainbow shoals in the Avon River
Fame-finned, Stratford-proud

On the bank a stage:
Thunderous hoofsounds and fertile winds

Kings swap masks with clowns
Stones de-claim their sermons

Brooks wax learned in running books
The midsummer is rank with rooks

And phantom Bottoms.
A stung Prince of Doubt wonders

Whether to be or not to bee
Cowards still dye many threads

Before their wool, the Badge of Brutus
Glowing famously on the chests of many friends

Othello, Moor or less,
Still more noble than nifty. . .

Those airy nothings still seed our spheres
Endowing every pulse with

Believed by many to be Shakespeare's birthday.

A local habitation
And *a name*

The sun rises, new, on this day
A soiree of songs inhabits the stars

Empire Day

(Martial music: harsh)

The bell commanded the school
Into neat, obedient lines
Our khaki uniforms shining
From the meticulous laundering

Of the previous day
Our finger nails pared
Our hair barbered in the stipulated
Prince-Herbert-on-Board style

The headmaster,
His shoe-and-stockings correct
A highway of a parting running
Dutifully through his salt-and-pepper hair

Cleared his voice and stood straight
Up like a pole
He extolled the virtues of Empire
The radiance of the Queen of England

Who was also our Queen
(Her mother who was also our mother)
Sovereign of our stars
The face on the coins

Which controlled our commerce

She owned the yams on our farms
She owned our cocoa and coffee and rubber
She owned the water in our lakes
She owned the mountains towering by the rivers

She owned the sky above our heads
She owned the land on which we stood
Her church was our church
Her god was our god

Her history was our history

The Band Master raised his stick
And the school erupted into song
First, "Rule Britannia"
Then, "God Save the King"

The Union Jack fluttered in the wind
Blue, red, and very white
The Headmaster stood at attention
Eyes closed, face wrinkled with reverence

He never knew when the midday sun
Suddenly vanished behind the clouds
And the heavens came down
In a voluminous hail of water...

Independence Day

(*Some anthem-like tune, a mix of heady high and tempered low*)

The cock which crowed in that day
Was stout, its throat powered
By a special thunder
The bell sounded different
The blackboard looked blacker
The lawns wore a different green
The teachers came to school
In their "Sunday bests"/ neatest smiles
The ubiquitous cane
Disappeared behind the cupboard

The sun that day wore anklebells
We heard the metallic
Music on our lines
The headmaster stepped forward
Briskly flicking his *agbada* sleeves
He saw us without his glasses
And could feel the fire in our eyes
"Today is Independence Day",
His voice rose to the listening skies
"From now on,
We make our own laws
Sing our own song
Live our own lives
So, brace up, boys and girls
Read your books
Grab your machetes
We have a country to build"

The band struck up a tune
The school exploded in joyous chorus
We danced through the streets
Draped in green-white-green
In the town center,
Just three stalls from the Post Office
We saw a marvelous sight

A big black man sat in the car
Where the dreaded D.O. used to sit
On his hands a pair of white gloves
On his head a whitened wig
He smiled and smiled and smiled
But we could not see his teeth

October was the month
The tenth link in the year's busy chain
The sun was blue and soft and kind

"Will you still be here tomorrow?", I asked,
But the Sun was too distant to hear my voice.

First Day of Spring

(for Mary Jay)

Crocuses croon
below my window

The tulip's full-throated laughter
breaks out beneath the leaves

Trees budding
Squirrels on board

Blossoms perfume the pavements
cherry and very merry

All around
growing things greet the earth

With magic
and risen roots

The sky inches quietly
towards the sun

Dewtaps on the hedges
the grass is singing again.

Jump Day*

The day springs forward
by one hour at dawn
the clock rolls on

with the giddy joy
of a schoolboy
that has just skipped a class

across the window
in the pensive garden
an infant foliage

turbans treetops,
olive this hour
and blissfully forgetful

Spring's heart
beats at a special rate
the birds are singing again.

Daylight-saving time, April 2005

Day of the Lily

This day hearkens to
the lyric of the lily
the soft, ethereal touch

Of petals on the rise
stamens
of unheard prayers

The butterfly's busy dalliance,
wings spread out
like rainbow bunting

In the wind.
Oh joyful moments
White, white teeth

In the green mouth
of the valley:
eloquence of the rain.

Questions

What are

dog days that cannot bark

lion days that cannot roar

ram days with broken horns

fish days that cannot swim

gold days that cannot glow

towncrier-days without a voice

temple days without a god...

Some days are a magnet that

cannot win the love of common metal

Sun on Roof

When I looked up today

The sun was dancing
on the roof

Its feet were made
of corrals

Its legs beams
from ancient forests

The drum spoke
in a dread-ful tongue

Its corrugated face
glittering in the heat

Membranes of the moon
wrapped up the daughter-drum

Quick on the stick
round on the ruse

Anklebells and arm rattles
waistbeads and rosary rounds

Hours leapt like lynxes
minutes swayed as if in trance

The sun danced on the roof
the house sang a hungry song

Hunger Days

seedless husks
vines in search of roots

meager grains
quarrelling in the bowl

the venison in the pot
has run off for deer life

the town's stomach has
gone behind its back

its intestines growling
like rattled serpents

dry days
deaf as dust

the clouds stub
a toe on a stony sky

and waste their charge
on shimmering shards

mornings break no fast
evenings go to bed

with straws
between their teeth

yet, in a land beyond the seas
dogs feast from golden plates

the cat's dinner
consumes a handsome fortune

Rich Day, Poor Day

Rich day
Poor day

Where are your empires
Where are your conquests

How many skulls
Pave the ground

On which
Your castle stands

Poor day
Rich day

Show me your pogroms
Show me your branded hours

Ocean floors white
With black bones

Scars so long
They stretch from

South
To North

I Know Days

I know of

days which kick
when cowed

demand
when remanded

love
when loathed

days which
wonder from the pack

put a sun
in nightly tunnels

pillory golden idols
for their greedy glitter

I know of days
which choose their (own) parents

Do Days

Days fly
We cannot see their wings

Days walk
On legs unseen

Days swim
In the season's eye

Days live on mists
And murmuring winds

Days know their room
In the house of the sun

Days dance on
The clock and its silver face

Days rush into marriage
With absent brides

Days speak
The hills echo their voices.

The Dial. . .

. . . this day
is on the melancholy democracy
of recurrent seasons

the equal agitation
of wounded moments
the un-harnessing of harassed instants

on the wizened tree
in the backyard of the day
leaves mope their dope

de-enfranchised birds un-
settle their nests, throats
rippling with striving songs

long, oh so long,
the road to /from Freedom's temple
thunderclaps of marching feet

here, then, the Song of the Soul
Fire of the Flower that
no waterhose can ever kill

Love Day

Light the fire
Stoke the flame
This day is the day
That love has chosen

The pigeon eyes the dove beneath the eaves
The buck tilts its ears towards the doe
Trees lock leaves with trees
In their green dance above the roofs

Hours embrace their minutes
Weeks wax strong on the passion
Of endless seasons. Drops of desire
Bloom into stirring seas

    This is the day

Of purple sighs and care-less laughters
Of long-missed songs and throbbing winds
There is a sparkle in the eye of the sun
The moon's cheek is a paradise of dimples

I Envy the Days

I envy the days
For the civility of their order

I have never heard Monday
Speak ill of Sunday

Have never heard Thursday grudge
Wednesday for its urn of ashes

Sunday never blames Saturday
For the wildness of its ways

Nor does Friday ever ridicule Tuesday
For being in the middle of nowhere

Each day has its own range
Knows its limits

No day has ever tried
To extend its hours

None has ever planted its flag
In its neighbour's garden

No day ever hassles the world
With the myth of a jealous god.

www.ingramcontent.com/pod-product-compliance
Lightning Source LLC
Chambersburg PA
CBHW011748220426
43669CB00020B/2949